THE
INQUISITEER

Editor: Erin Adams
Design: Eva Lineberger

AUTHOR

Luke Baker is a writer living in Atlanta with a passion for wielding words and whimsy to help people connect with themselves and their neighbor. He believes most good things — like this book — take time, teamwork, and empathetic curiosity.

CONTENTS

"

JUDGE A MAN BY HIS
QUESTIONS RATHER
THAN HIS ANSWERS.

−VOLTAIRE

ANIMALS

WHICH
ANIMAL DO
YOU
THINK IS
MISUNDERSTOOD?

WHICH
ANIMAL WOULD
YOU
LIKE TO SEE
IN THE
WILD?

IF YOU COULD
CHOOSE
ONE
ANIMAL
TO MAKE A
DIFFERENT
ANIMAL NOISE,
WHICH
COMBINATION
WOULD YOU
CHOOSE?

WHICH

    ANIMAL

        DO YOU

WISH

    DIDN'T

    EXIST?

IF YOU
COULD
BRING BACK AN
EXTINCT
ANIMAL,
WHICH ONE
WOULD YOU
CHOOSE?

IF YOU COULD

TALK

TO ONE

ANIMAL,

WHICH WOULD

YOU

CHOOSE?

ANNOYANCES

WHAT IS

ONE WORD

YOU WISH

DIDN'T

EXIST?

WHAT'S

YOUR

BIGGEST

PET PEEVE?

WHAT MAKES

YOU

ANGRY?

WHAT'S A

BAD HABIT

YOU WISH

YOU COULD

BREAK

TODAY?

WHAT

DO YOU

COMPLAIN

ABOUT

THE MOST?

WHAT
QUESTION
DO YOU
HATE
BEING
ASKED?

ART

WHEN HAVE
YOU BEEN THE
MOST
MOVED
BY A
PIECE OF
ART?

IF YOU

COULD

PERFECTLY

RECREATE

ONE PIECE

OF ART,

WHAT WOULD

IT BE?

WHAT IS YOUR
FAVORITE
TYPE OF
ART?

IF YOU COULD

HAVE ANY

PIECE OF

ART

HANGING OVER

YOUR MANTLE,

WHAT

WOULD IT BE?

WHICH PIECE OF
ART
WOULD YOU
MOST WANT TO
SEE IN
PERSON?

BOOKS

IF YOU COULD
BRING ONE
CHARACTER
TO LIFE
FROM A BOOK,
WHO
WOULD IT BE?

WHAT BOOK
HAVE YOU
RECOMMENDED
THE MOST?

WHAT WOULD

BE THE

TITLE

OF YOUR

AUTOBIOGRAPHY?

IF YOU HAD TO
WRITE A BOOK,
WHAT
WOULD YOU WRITE
ABOUT?

WHAT FICTIONAL
BOOK
CHARACTER
DO YOU RELATE TO
THE MOST?

WHAT'S A
MOVIE
THAT YOU
WISH
WAS BASED ON
A BOOK?

WHAT'S THE

BEST BOOK

YOU'VE

NEVER

FINISHED?

WHAT

BOOK

HAS MADE THE

BIGGEST IMPACT

ON YOUR

LIFE?

CELEBRITIES

IF YOU GOT TO
CHOOSE A
CELEBRITY
TO BE YOUR
MENTOR,
WHO WOULD IT BE?

WHO DO YOU
WISH WAS
LESS
FAMOUS?

FOR WHICH
CELEBRITY
FAMILY
WOULD YOU LIKE
TO BE THE
BUTLER?

WHO IS SOMEONE
THAT YOU
HAVEN'T MET
WHO HAS HAD THE
GREATEST
IMPACT
ON YOUR
LIFE?

WHAT WOULD
YOU WANT TO BE
FAMOUS
FOR?

WHO IS THE
MOST FAMOUS
PERSON YOU HAVE
EVER MET?

IF YOU COULD TAKE
THREE
CELEBRITIES
TO A PARTY,
WHO WOULD
YOU TAKE?

HAVE YOU
EXPERIENCED
YOUR
15 MINUTES
OF FAME?

COMMUNICATION

WHAT
EMOJI
DO YOU WISH
EXISTED?

WHAT'S THE
BEST
PHONE CALL
YOU'VE EVER
RECEIVED?

WHAT
OLD-FASHIONED
FORM OF
COMMUNICATION
DO YOU WISH
WAS STILL
COMMONLY
PRACTICED?

IF YOU COULD

ONLY HAVE

FIVE CONTACTS

IN YOUR PHONE,

WHO WOULD

THEY BE?

WHAT FORM OF
COMMUNICATION
DO YOU WISH
DIDN'T
EXIST?

WHAT'S THE

BEST SPEECH

YOU'VE

EVER

GIVEN?

WHAT
LANGUAGE
DO YOU WISH YOU
COULD SPEAK
FLUENTLY?

COVID-19

WHAT
    HABIT
DID YOU DEVELOP
DURING
        COVID-19
    THAT YOU'RE
STILL
    PRACTICING?

WHAT DID YOU

LEARN

ABOUT YOURSELF

DURING

COVID-19?

DID YOU
PICK UP A
NEW HOBBY
DURING
COVID-19?

WHAT WAS THE
HARDEST PART
OF COVID-19
FOR YOU?

WHAT WAS
ONE OF THE
MOST
JOYFUL
MOMENTS
YOU HAD DURING
COVID-19?

IF YOU COULD HAVE
TOLD YOURSELF
ONE THING
BEFORE
THE PANDEMIC
TO HELP
YOU PREPARE FOR IT,
WHAT WOULD
IT HAVE BEEN?

WHAT'S
ONE THING
YOU'RE PROUD OF
FROM THE
COVID-19
SEASON?

CROWDSOURCED

WHAT'S YOUR

STORY?

— ANA M.

WHAT'S THE

    CRAZIEST THING

YOU'VE

    EVER

        SEEN?

    — JAKE B.

WHEN IN LIFE DO
YOU FEEL
MOST
LOVED?

– JOSH K.

WHAT IS YOUR

HEAVEN

WALK-IN

SONG?

— KATIE K.

WHAT'S YOUR
FAVORITE STORY
TO TELL FROM YOUR
LIFE?

— JOHN V.

WHAT IS THE

BOOK

YOU'VE GIFTED

THE MOST?

— LEIGHTON C.

WHAT
IS SOMETHING
INTERESTING
YOU'VE RECENTLY
LEARNED?

— ERIN H.

WHAT'S YOUR
FAVORITE
SMELL?

— SARAH J.

WHAT'S THE
BEST ADVICE
YOUR
GRANDMOTHER
GAVE YOU?

— HANNAH F.

IF YOU COULD

CHANGE

ONE THING

IN YOUR LIFE

RIGHT NOW,

WHAT WOULD IT BE?

— TODD L.

IF YOU COULD ONLY
KEEP AND READ
ONE BOOK
FOR THE
REST OF YOUR LIFE,
WHAT WOULD
IT BE?

— ANDREA P.

DEATH

WHAT'S

ONE THING

YOU WANT TO

ACCOMPLISH

BY THE

END

OF YOUR LIFE?

WHAT

DO YOU

WANT YOUR

TOMBSTONE

TO SAY?

HOW WOULD YOU

PREFER

TO

DIE?

WHAT DO YOU
WISH
HAPPENED TO PEOPLE
AFTER THEY
DIED?

WHAT DO YOU
WANT
YOUR LEGACY
TO BE?

DRIVING

WHEN HAVE YOU
BEEN THE
MOST SCARED
WHILE
DRIVING?

WHAT'S YOUR
DREAM
VEHICLE?

IF YOU HAD TO
DRIVE
ACROSS
THE COUNTRY
VIA ANY MODE OF
TRANSPORTATION,
WHAT WOULD
IT BE?

WHAT MAKES YOU
ANGRY
WHILE DRIVING?

WHAT ELEMENT
DO YOU THINK
SHOULD BE
INCORPORATED
IN THE
DRIVER'S TEST?

WHAT
WOULD IT TAKE FOR
YOU TO
PICK UP A
HITCHHIKER?

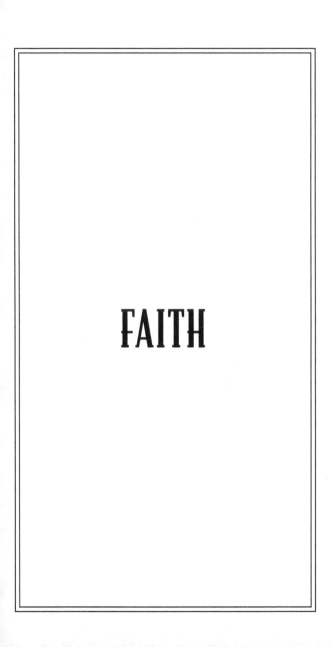

FAITH

WHAT

COMES TO

MIND

WHEN YOU THINK OF

GOD?

WHEN

DID YOUR

FAITH

MAKE THE

BIGGEST SHIFT?

WHAT
IS SOMETHING
HARD FOR YOU
TO
BELIEVE?

WHAT
WOULD HAVE TO
HAPPEN
TO MAKE YOU
BELIEVE IN A
HIGHER POWER?

WHAT WOULD
HAVE TO
HAPPEN
TO MAKE YOU
STOP
BELIEVING IN A
HIGHER POWER?

IF YOU COULD ASK

GOD

ONE

QUESTION,

WHAT WOULD IT BE?

FAMILY

WHAT'S AN
ATTRIBUTE FROM
EACH
OF YOUR PARENTS
THAT YOU'D
LIKE TO
EMBODY?

WHAT'S BEEN
YOUR
FAVORITE
FAMILY VACATION?

WHAT'S YOUR
FAVORITE
FAMILY TRADITION?

HOW ARE YOU
MOST SIMILAR
TO YOUR
PARENTS?

WHAT WOULD YOUR
FAMILY
SAY
IS YOUR
BIGGEST
WEAKNESS?

FASHION

WHAT'S

YOUR

FAVORITE

ARTICLE

OF CLOTHING?

IF YOU COULD

COMPLETELY

END

ONE FASHION TREND,

WHAT WOULD

IT BE?

WHAT'S A
PIECE OF CLOTHING
THAT YOU'VE
WANTED
FOR A WHILE,
BUT DON'T WANT TO
SPEND THE
MONEY TO BUY?

WHAT

COLOR

DO YOU THINK

LOOKS

BEST ON YOU?

WHAT WAS YOUR
STYLE
LIKE IN
HIGH SCHOOL?

WHAT HAS BEEN

YOUR

WORST

FASHION DECISION?

IF MONEY WERE
NO OBJECT,
WHERE
WOULD YOU BUY
YOUR CLOTHES?

FOOD

IF YOU HAD TO EAT
ONE FOOD
FOR THE
REST OF
YOUR LIFE,
WHAT WOULD IT BE?

WHAT'S YOUR
MOST
MEMORABLE
MEAL?

IF YOU COULD COOK
ONE FOOD
BETTER THAN
ANYONE ELSE IN
THE
WORLD,
WHAT WOULD IT BE?

WHAT'S A FOOD YOU
WISH YOU
    ENJOYED
MORE?

IF YOU
WERE STARTING
YOUR
OWN
RESTAURANT,
WHAT KIND OF
FOOD
WOULD YOU SERVE?

WHAT'S YOUR

FAVORITE

HOME-COOKED

MEAL?

WHAT MEAL
HAVE YOU RECENTLY
HAD THAT YOU
WOULD RATE A
10
OUT OF
10?

FRIENDS

WHAT DO YOU

LOOK FOR

IN A

FRIEND?

IF YOU HAD TO
NAME
YOUR
CHILD
AFTER A FRIEND,
WHO WOULD
IT BE?

WHAT

FOUR FRIENDS

WOULD BE ON THE

FACE

OF YOUR

MOUNT

RUSHMORE?

HOW
WOULD YOUR
BEST FRIENDS
DESCRIBE
YOU?

WHAT IS YOUR
FAVORITE
QUALITY
IN YOUR
BEST FRIEND?

GAMES

WHAT
CHILDREN'S GAME
DO YOU WISH
ADULTS PLAYED
MORE OFTEN?

WHAT'S YOUR
FAVORITE
BOARD GAME?

IF YOU HAD TO
INVENT A
    GAME SHOW,
WHAT WOULD IT BE?

WHAT'S A

POPULAR GAME

THAT YOU'VE NEVER

REALLY

LIKED?

WHEN HAVE YOU
GOTTEN THE
MOST UPSET
OVER A GAME?

GIVING

IF YOU WERE TO
WIN THE
LOTTERY,
WHAT IS THE
FIRST THING
YOU WOULD BUY FOR
SOMEONE
ELSE?

WHAT IS THE
        WORST GIFT
YOU'VE GIVEN TO
SOMEONE?

IF YOU HAD TO GIVE

EVERYONE

THE

SAME THING

FOR THEIR BIRTHDAY,

WHAT WOULD IT

BE?

WHAT IS SOMETHING

YOU

WISH YOU

COULD MAKE COME

TRUE

FOR SOMEONE

ELSE?

IF YOU HAD A
MILLION
DOLLARS
TO JUST GIVE AWAY,
HOW
WOULD YOU DO IT?

WHAT WAS YOUR
FAVORITE GIFT
THAT YOU BOUGHT
FOR
SOMEONE
ELSE?

HISTORY

IF YOU COULD GO

BACK IN TIME

AND ALTER

ONE

HISTORICAL EVENT,

WHAT

WOULD IT BE?

IN WHAT
ERA
DO YOU WISH YOU
COULD LIVE FOR
ONE
YEAR?

IF YOU COULD
EXPERIENCE A
MOMENT
IN ANOTHER
PERSON'S LIFE,
WHO
WOULD YOU CHOOSE
AND WHICH
MOMENT
WOULD IT BE?

WHICH
HISTORICAL
FIGURE
DO YOU WISH WAS
STILL
ALIVE?

IF YOU COULD GO
BACK IN
TIME
AND
OBSERVE
ONE
HISTORICAL EVENT,
WHAT WOULD IT
BE?

WHICH
STORY
IN HISTORY
MOST
FASCINATES
YOU?

HOLIDAYS

IF YOU HAD TO
MAKE A
                HOLIDAY
CELEBRATING
        ANYTHING,
            WHAT
WOULD IT BE?

WHAT'S A
HOLIDAY THAT
YOU
DON'T
ENJOY
CELEBRATING?

WHAT'S YOUR
FAVORITE
HOLIDAY?

WHAT'S THE
BEST
CHRISTMAS GIFT
YOU'VE
EVER
RECEIVED?

GROWING UP,

WHAT DID YOU

DRESS UP

AS FOR

HALLOWEEN?

WHAT'S YOUR
FAVORITE DISH
OF A
THANKSGIVING
MEAL?

WHAT
DO YOU WANT TO BE
NEW
ABOUT YOU
BY THIS
NEW
YEAR'S?

HOME

WHAT'S YOUR

FAVORITE SPACE

IN YOUR

HOUSE?

WHAT

    PART

OF A

      HOUSE

DO YOU THINK IS

    UNDERRATED?

WHAT DO
YOU THINK
MAKES
GREAT
HOSPITALITY?

HOW MANY

DIFFERENT

HOMES

HAVE YOU LIVED IN?

WHAT'S YOUR

FAVORITE

PART

ABOUT YOUR

HOMETOWN?

IF YOU COULD MAKE
ONE CHANGE
TO YOUR
CURRENT HOME,
WHAT
WOULD IT BE?

KNOWLEDGE

WHAT'S A
SUBJECT
YOU WOULD LIKE TO
SEE
TAUGHT IN
EVERY
SCHOOL?

IF YOU COULD KNOW

EVERYTHING

ABOUT

ONE SPECIFIC

TOPIC,

WHAT

WOULD IT BE?

WHAT IS SOMETHING
YOU
KNOW
            FOR
    SURE?

WHAT'S

    SOMETHING

YOU WOULD LIKE TO

HAVE

    MEMORIZED?

IF YOU GOT TO
TEACH A CLASS,
WHAT
WOULD IT BE ABOUT?

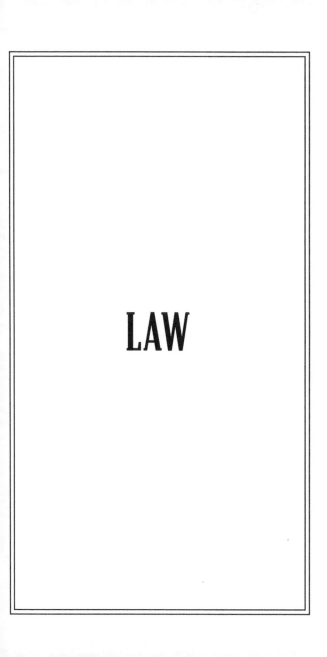

LAW

IF YOU COULD
COMMIT
ONE CRIME
WITHOUT
SUFFERING
THE CONSEQUENCES,
WHAT
WOULD IT BE?

WHAT ARE YOU

MOST LIKELY

TO GET

ARRESTED

FOR

SOMEDAY?

WHAT

LAW

DO YOU WISH YOU

COULD

REPEAL

RIGHT

NOW?

WHAT
LAW
DO YOU WISH YOU
COULD
ESTABLISH
RIGHT
NOW?

IF YOU HAD TO
MAKE A LIVING
DOING AN
ILLEGAL
ACTIVITY,
WHAT WOULD IT BE?

WHAT

   COMMONLY

   BROKEN

         LAW

MAKES YOU WANT TO

MAKE A

   CITIZEN'S

         ARREST?

MEMORIES

IF YOU COULD RELIVE
ONE MOMENT
OF YOUR
LIFE,
JUST TO
EXPERIENCE
IT AGAIN,
WHAT WOULD IT BE?

WHEN
HAVE YOU FELT THE
MOST
LOVED?

WHAT

DAY

WILL YOU

NEVER

FORGET?

WHEN

WAS THE

LAST TIME

SOMEONE OR

SOMETHING

EXCEEDED

YOUR

EXPECTATIONS?

WHAT'S A
PERSONAL
PAINFUL
MOMENT
THAT YOU
WOULDN'T REDO
IF GIVEN THE
CHANCE?

IF YOU COULD

ALTER

ONE EVENT

IN YOUR LIFE,

WHAT WOULD IT BE?

WHEN

WAS A TIME

YOU WISH

YOU COULD HAVE

BEEN IN

TWO PLACES

AT ONCE?

WHEN WAS THE

LAST TIME

YOU WERE

SPEECHLESS?

WHAT'S BEEN

YOUR

BEST BIRTHDAY?

WHAT'S THE
MOST EXCITED
YOU'VE BEEN FOR
SOMEONE
ELSE?

WHAT'S YOUR

FIRST MEMORY?

MOVIES

IF THERE WAS A
MOVIE
ABOUT YOU,
WHO
WOULD PLAY
YOU?

WHAT WAS THE
LAST MOVIE
THAT MADE YOU
CRY?

IF YOU WERE STUCK

ON AN ISLAND

BY YOURSELF

AND COULD ONLY

HAVE

THREE

MOVIES,

WHICH

WOULD YOU

CHOOSE?

IF YOU GOT TO BE

ON

SET

FOR THE FILMING OF

ONE MOVIE,

WHAT WOULD IT BE?

IF YOU HAD TO
NAME YOUR
CHILD
AFTER A
MOVIE
CHARACTER,
WHO WOULD IT BE?

WHAT BOOK
DO YOU WISH
WAS ALSO A
MOVIE?

WHAT'S

ONE MOVIE

YOU WISH YOU

WOULD HAVE

NEVER

SEEN?

IF YOU COULD
REWRITE A
SCENE
FROM A
MOVIE,
WHAT SCENE
WOULD IT BE?

WHICH
CLASSIC
MOVIE
HAVE YOU
NEVER SEEN?

WHAT'S THE

WORST

MOVIE

YOU'VE EVER

SEEN?

MUSIC

IF YOU COULD
SING
ONE SONG
PERFECTLY,
WHICH WOULD YOU
CHOOSE?

IF YOU HAD A
"WALK IN"
SONG
THAT PLAYED
EVERY TIME YOU
ENTERED A
NEW PLACE,
WHAT WOULD IT BE?

WHICH
BAND,
ALIVE OR DEAD,
DO YOU WISH YOU
COULD SEE
PERFORM
LIVE?

WHAT
SONG
HAS BROUGHT YOU
TO TEARS OR
GOOSEBUMPS?

WHAT

BAND OR ARTIST

DO YOU THINK IS

OVERRATED?

WHAT'S A SONG
THAT YOU
          LIKE,
BUT STILL
     DON'T
          KNOW
WHAT THE
     LYRICS MEAN?

WHO
WOULD YOU WANT
TO
SING A SONG
ABOUT YOUR
LIFE?

IF YOU HAD TO
LISTEN TO
THREE ARTISTS
FOR THE
REST OF
YOUR LIFE,
WHO WOULD
THEY BE?

WHICH
ARTIST
DO YOU WISH HAD
NEVER
MADE IT ON THE
MUSIC SCENE?

WHAT
MUSICAL GENRE
DO YOU WISH
DIDN'T EXIST?

NATURE

IF YOU COULD MAKE
IT
    RAIN
ONE THING,
WHAT WOULD IT BE?

WHAT'S YOUR
FAVORITE KIND OF
WEATHER?

IF YOU COULD
WITNESS
ONE TYPE OF
NATURAL
DISASTER,
WHAT WOULD IT BE?

WHEN HAVE YOU

BEEN MOST IN

AWE

OF

NATURE?

WHEN HAVE YOU
MOST
FEARED
SOMETHING IN
NATURE?

WHAT'S A
NATURAL
LANDMARK
THAT YOU WOULD
LOVE
TO VISIT?

WHAT'S YOUR
FAVORITE
FLOWER?

QUESTION ASKING

IF YOU COULD ASK

FOR THE

ABSOLUTE

TRUTH

FOR ONE QUESTION

AND BE GUARANTEED

THE ANSWER,

WHAT WOULD YOU

ASK?

WHAT IS
    ONE QUESTION
THAT YOU HAVE
        REGRETTED
ASKING?

WHAT'S A
QUESTION YOU
WISH
WAS ASKED IN EVERY
JOB
INTERVIEW?

WHAT'S ONE OF
THE

BEST
QUESTIONS
YOU'VE EVER BEEN
ASKED?

WHAT'S ONE
QUESTION
YOU WISH
PEOPLE ASKED
MORE
OFTEN?

WHAT

QUESTION

HAVE YOU REGRETTED

NOT

ASKING?

IF YOU ONLY HAD

ONE QUESTION

TO ASK ON A

FIRST

DATE,

WHAT WOULD IT BE?

WHAT
QUESTION DO YOU
ASK
YOURSELF
THE MOST?

WHAT

QUESTION

DO YOU

HATE?

ROMANCE

WHAT'S YOUR MOST
AWKWARD
DATE
STORY?

WHAT

SPECIFIC

QUALITIES

MAKE YOU

ROMANTICALLY

ATTRACTED

TO AN INDIVIDUAL?

WHEN DID YOU
FIRST
REALIZE
YOU WERE
EXPERIENCING
LOVE?

WHAT'S YOUR

DREAM

DATE?

WHO WAS YOUR
FIRST
KISS?

WHAT IS YOUR

MOST

UNFORGETTABLE

DATE?

WHAT HAS BEEN THE
MOST
MEMORABLE
WEDDING
YOU'VE ATTENDED?

SLEEP

WHAT'S THE

MOST

BIZZARE

DREAM YOU'VE

EVER HAD?

WHAT

   ACTIVITY

(BESIDES SLEEPING)

IS MOST

   RESTFUL

FOR YOU?

WHEN
WERE YOU
SO EXCITED
FOR THE
NEXT DAY
THAT IT WAS
DIFFICULT TO
SLEEP?

WHAT

    FEAR

KEEPS YOU UP AT

    NIGHT?

WHERE IS THE

MOST

UNUSUAL PLACE

YOU'VE FALLEN

ASLEEP?

WHAT
IS YOUR
MOST FREQUENT
RECURRING
DREAM?

SPORTS

WHAT

SPORTING

EVENT

WOULD YOU LOVE TO

ATTEND?

IF YOU HAD

FOUR YEARS

TO TRAIN FOR AN

OLYMPICS,

WHICH TEAM WOULD

YOU HAVE THE

BEST SHOT OF

MAKING?

WHAT WOULD YOU

GIVE

TO SEE YOUR

TEAM

WIN IT

ALL?

WHAT

SPORTS

MOMENT

WILL YOU

NEVER

FORGET?

AS A

CHILD,
WHO WAS YOUR
FAVORITE
ATHLETE?

IN WHICH

SPORT

DO YOU WISH

YOU

EXCELLED?

WHAT

UNUSUAL SPORT

WOULD YOU LIKE TO

SEE IN THE

OLYMPICS?

SUPERPOWERS

WHAT IS THE

MOST

USELESS

SUPERPOWER

YOU CAN THINK OF?

IF YOU COULD

TELEPORT

ONCE A MONTH,

BUT COULD ONLY GO

TO

ONE PLACE,

WHERE

WOULD IT BE?

WHAT

SUPERPOWER

DO YOU WISH

EVERYONE

HAD?

IF YOU COULD
CHOOSE TO HAVE
ONE
SUPERPOWER,
WHAT WOULD IT BE?

IF YOU COULD BE
INVISIBLE
FOR ONE
DAY,
WHAT WOULD YOU
DO?

WITH WHICH

SUPERHERO

COULD YOU SEE

YOURSELF

BEING

GOOD FRIENDS?

TACTICS

IF YOU HAD TO HIDE

FROM

PRIVATE

DETECTIVES

FOR AS LONG AS

POSSIBLE, HOW

WOULD YOU

DO IT?

IF YOU HAD TO
CONVINCE A
STRANGER TO
MARRY
YOU
BY THE END OF THE
DAY,
HOW WOULD YOU
GO ABOUT IT?

IF YOU HAD TO
THROW A PARTY FOR
COMPLETE
STRANGERS,
WHAT TYPE OF
PARTY
WOULD IT BE AND
HOW
WOULD YOU GET
THEM THERE?

IF YOU HAD TO
TRAVEL
ACROSS THE
COUNTRY WITH ONLY
$100,
HOW WOULD
YOU DO IT?

IF YOU HAD
15 MINUTES
IN A WALMART TO
SEE HOW MUCH
MONETARY
DAMAGE YOU COULD
CAUSE,
WHAT WOULD
BE YOUR APPROACH?

IF YOUR LIFE
DEPENDED
ON YOU RAISING
ONE MILLION
DOLLARS IN A
WEEK,
HOW
WOULD YOU DO IT?

TECHNOLOGY

WHAT

APP

DO YOU WISH

EXISTED?

IF YOU COULD HAVE
PREVENTED
　　　ONE THING
FROM BEING
　　　　　INVENTED,
WHAT WOULD IT BE?

WHAT DO YOU
HOPE
WILL BE THE
GREATEST
TECHNOLOGICAL
DISCOVERY
FIFTY YEARS
FROM NOW?

WHAT
      SITE
DO YOU VISIT
      MOST OFTEN?

WHAT COMMON
ACTIVITY WOULD YOU
LIKE TO SEE
    ROBOTS
START DOING
INSTEAD OF
        HUMANS?

IF YOU HAD TO
START A
PODCAST,
WHAT
WOULD IT BE ABOUT?

IF YOU COULD ONLY
HAVE
ONE
SOCIAL MEDIA
PLATFORM,
WHICH WOULD YOU
CHOOSE?

THOUGHTS

WHAT'S SOMETHING
OUR SOCIETY
DOES OR BELIEVES
THAT PEOPLE WILL
ONE DAY LOOK BACK
AND ASK,
"WHAT WERE
THEY
THINKING?"

WHAT DO YOU

    THINK ABOUT

IN THE

       SHOWER?

WHAT'S SOMETHING

YOU

THINK ABOUT

THAT MOST PEOPLE

PROBABLY

DON'T?

WHAT'S THE
FIRST
ADJECTIVE
THAT COMES TO
MIND WHEN YOU
READ YOUR
NAME?

WHAT'S TYPICALLY
YOUR
    FIRST THOUGHT
WHEN YOU
    WAKE UP IN THE
    MORNING?

TRAVEL

WHAT'S ONE
LANDMARK
YOU WISH YOU
COULD VISIT
RIGHT
NOW?

IF YOU COULD
LIVE FOR
A YEAR
IN ANOTHER
COUNTRY,
WHERE
WOULD YOU GO?

WHAT'S A
NON-ESSENTIAL
ITEM
THAT YOU ALWAYS
TAKE
WITH YOU
WHEN YOU
TRAVEL?

WHERE DO YOU
WISH
BLACK HOLES
WOULD
LEAD?

WHAT'S YOUR
DREAM
VACATION?

IF YOU HAD A WEEK
TO
ROAD-TRIP
SOMEWHERE,
WHERE
WOULD YOU
GO?

WHAT

CITY

HAVE YOU BEEN

WANTING TO

VISIT?

WORK

WHAT'S A JOB YOU
WOULD
GLADLY DO
FOR FREE
FOR THE REST OF
YOUR
LIFE?

WHAT IS YOUR
FAVORITE
QUALITY IN
YOUR
FAVORITE
BOSS?

IF YOU HAD TO
START YOUR
OWN
BUSINESS
TODAY,
WHAT WOULD IT BE?

WHAT'S

    ONE JOB YOU

        WOULDN'T

DO

FOR ALL THE

        MONEY

IN THE WORLD?

IF YOU COULD
CHANGE
ONE
THING ABOUT YOUR
CURRENT
JOB,
WHAT WOULD IT BE?

WHAT WAS YOUR
FIRST
JOB?

IF YOUR COMPANY
PASSED OUT
SUPERLATIVES,
WHAT WOULD
YOURS BE?

WHAT'S A
JOB YOU WOULD
LIKE TO DO,
BUT WILL PROBABLY
NEVER
PURSUE?

WHAT ABOUT YOUR

CURRENT

JOB

MAKES YOU COME

ALIVE?

WORLDWIDE

IF YOU HAD A
MICROPHONE
THAT WOULD
ECHO AROUND THE
WHOLE WORLD,
AND YOU WERE
ALLOWED TO SAY
THREE
WORDS,
WHAT WOULD YOU
SAY?

IF YOU COULD PICK

ONE THING

TO BE THE

BEST

IN THE WORLD AT,

WHAT

WOULD IT BE?

IF YOU COULD GIVE
EVERYONE
IN THE WORLD ONE
MATERIALISTIC
THING,
WHAT WOULD IT BE?

IF YOU WERE DOING
SHOW-AND-TELL
IN FRONT OF THE
WORLD,
WHAT
ITEM
WOULD YOU
SHARE?

IF YOU HAD TO
ATTEMPT
BREAKING A
WORLD
RECORD,
WHICH ONE WOULD
IT BE?

WITH YOUR
CURRENT
SKILLS,
WHAT'S
ONE THING
YOU COULD
ACTUALLY BE THE
BEST IN THE
WORLD
AT?

RANDOM

IF YOU COULD SPEND
A DAY
WITH
ONE PERSON,
ALIVE OR
DEAD,
WHO WOULD IT BE?

WHAT'S A
DREAM OF
YOURS THAT YOU'RE
NOT
PURSUING?

IF YOU HAD TO
GET A
TATTOO,
WHAT WOULD IT BE?

IF YOU COULD MAKE
ONE
MYTHICAL
        CREATURE
COME TO
            LIFE,
WHAT WOULD IT BE?

WHAT

    CLICHE SAYING

DO YOU

    DISAGREE

        WITH?

WHAT'S A
CHARACTERISTIC
OF A
CHILD
THAT YOU THINK
WOULD BE GOOD
FOR
ADULTS TO
HAVE?

ON WHAT

GAME SHOW

WOULD YOU LIKE TO

BE A

CONTESTANT?

IF YOU HAD TO
CHANGE YOUR
NAME,
WHAT
WOULD YOU
CHANGE IT TO?

WHAT IS ONE
NON-TYPICAL
THING
THAT YOU WANT
IN YOUR
HOUSE?

WHEN WAS A

TIME YOU

CRIED

FROM

HAPPINESS?

IF YOU HAD TO GO

THE

   REST OF YOUR

     LIFE

ONLY SEEING

   ONE COLOR,

WHAT WOULD IT BE?

WHAT

    CONSPIRACY

      THEORY

DO YOU

    WISH

WAS

      TRUE?

IF YOU HAD TO
BET
ALL OF YOUR
MONEY
ON SOMETHING
TOMORROW,
WHAT WOULD IT BE?

WHAT DO YOU

WISH

YOU DID

LESS OFTEN

IN LIFE?

IF YOU COULD
NOMINATE
ONE
PERSON
TO RUN FOR
PRESIDENT,
WHO WOULD IT BE?

WHAT MAKES

YOU COME

ALIVE?

IF YOU COULD SPEND
ONE DAY
AS ANOTHER
PERSON,
WHO WOULD IT BE?

WHAT'S AN

INTEREST

YOU

WISH

YOU HAD TIME TO

PURSUE?

WHAT STORE WOULD
YOU WORK AT
PART-TIME
IN ORDER TO
RECEIVE THE
EMPLOYEE
DISCOUNT?

IF YOU HAD AN

EXTRA

HOUR

IN YOUR DAY, HOW

WOULD YOU

USE IT?

WHAT DO YOU
THINK IS
OVERRATED
IN OUR SOCIETY?

IF YOU COULD GET

ONE THING FOR

FREE

FOR THE REST OF

YOUR

LIFE,

WHAT WOULD IT BE?

WHAT WOULD THOSE

WHO

DISLIKE YOU

SAY ABOUT

YOU?

WHAT PIECE OF
ADVICE WILL YOU
NEVER
FORGET?

WHO'S SOMEBODY
OF A DIFFERENT
RACE AND
GENDER
THAN YOU THAT YOU
ADMIRE?

WHAT ARE YOU
MOST EXCITED
ABOUT FOR THE NEXT
FIVE YEARS
OF YOUR
LIFE?

WHAT'S SOMETHING
YOU THINK
SHOULD BE ON
EVERYONE'S
BUCKET LIST?

ON WHAT

TV SHOW

WOULD YOU LIKE TO

HAVE BEEN

AN

ACTOR?

WHAT IS YOUR

LIFE

SLOGAN?

WHAT

ADVICE

WOULD YOU GIVE

YOUR

YOUNGER

SELF?

WHAT'S A
MISCONCEPTION
THAT
PEOPLE HAVE
ABOUT
YOU?

IF YOU'RE STARTING

A TALK

SHOW

AND CAN HOST ANY

LIVING PERSON,

WHO WOULD BE

ON THE

FIRST EPISODE?

IF YOU HAD ALL THE

COURAGE

IN THE

WORLD,

WHAT WOULD YOU

DO?

WHAT'S

ONE

HOBBY

THAT YOU

DON'T

UNDERSTAND?

WHAT DO YOU

THINK IS

UNDERRATED

IN OUR SOCIETY?

WHAT'S THE

BEST

PRANK

YOU'VE EVER BEEN A

PART OF?

WHO'S YOUR

FAVORITE

STORYTELLER?

WHAT'S A
MISTAKE
THAT EVERYONE
SHOULD
MAKE?

IF YOU HAD TO
WALK AROUND WITH
A
PERSONAL
WARNING
LABEL,
WHAT WOULD IT SAY?

WHAT

SUPERLATIVE

WOULD YOU WIN IN

THIS

SEASON

OF LIFE?

WHICH OF YOUR

FIVE

SENSES

IS THE

STRONGEST?

WHEN WAS THE
LAST TIME
YOU WERE MOVED
TO
TEARS?

WHEN
DO YOU FEEL
MOST
CONFIDENT?

WHAT DO YOU
WISH YOU DID
MORE
OFTEN IN
LIFE?

WHAT'S YOUR
FAVORITE
TIME
OF THE
DAY?

WHERE

DO YOU

GO

WHEN YOU WANT TO

GET

AWAY?

WHAT

WORD

DO YOU HAVE A

DIFFICULT TIME

SAYING?

WHAT'S YOUR

FAVORITE

QUOTE?

HAVE YOU EVER
COLLECTED
ANYTHING?

WHAT MAKES YOUR

GOOD DAY

A

GOOD

DAY?